T0197121

Chants of *Euphoria*

Cyril Oghomeh

authorHOUSE®

AuthorHouse™
1663 Liberty Drive
Bloomington, IN 47403
www.authorhouse.com
Phone: 833-262-8899

Published by AuthorHouse 12/22/2022

ISBN: 978-1-6655-7554-6 (sc)
ISBN: 978-1-6655-7553-9 (e)

Library of Congress Control Number: 2022921001

Print information available on the last page.

Contents

Dedication

In Loving memory of my father - Venerable Michael .I. Oghomeh

Acknowledgement

My profound thanks go to my amazing mother Susannah Oghomeh. From the bottom of my heart, I wish to express my gratitude for your requital of love, support and prayers during the development of this book. Also, to my wife Yasmaine, for putting a permanent smile on my face and giving my life a new meaning. My thanks also go to all my children and family members for their undying love; I draw so much courage, strength and inspiration from you all. Finally, to my friends and all lovers of poetry in the world, I say Thank You.

Introduction

My new oeuvre of poems – *Chants of Euphoria*, takes love language and romance deeper, and sets the reader to discover the life - transforming scenes, travels, rich cuisines, and fine monuments enjoyed all around the world.

Every size and depth of my life experiences, involving my relationships and marriages, both the bad and the good one are talked about in a manner that keeps the reader sometimes guessing, dialoguing, and at times conversing with themselves. The poems are well layered with witty innuendos and some offer advice in serious conversations about gun violence, death, grief, declaration of love and faith. The poems offers advice on finding and how to stay devoted in a relationship. Everything imaginable and intangible that a lover can use to show his or her heart's desire for a lasting commitment to endure is richly seen here. Also, many of the poems are romantic ballads with great settings, and they are informative and educational and open up conversations about some societal issues in a very entertaining and positive way.

Other poems pay tribute and talk about some old artistes and their classic songs; like Who Do You Love (Bernard Wright), The Warrior (Osibisa), Beauty is Only Skin Deep (The Temptations), Cruising (Smokey Robinson) and At Last (Etta James). The songs are described in a pleasurable manner so that it soughs through the readers' mind, feelings, thoughts and emotions, even making you ache for physical touch or caress from your loved one. Most of the lines of my poems are lyrically inclined, and it's infused with fresh passion. The reader is easily aroused by the simple objective and subject being described.

My Darling - Hors d'oeuvre

My darling, please taste the semblance to your attributes from my Hors d'oeuvre

They are little slices of my effects served on doilies to you for your russet love,

I must acknowledge that your love is magical and my Hors d'oeuvre is what you deserve

That's why I took up this quest believing the purest of my commitment came from above.

I'm giving you the best of my inkling for you to savor, just like what your pristine touches have done to my body over the years.

I have the purest of intents when I share my committal and hope of building a future with you

I can continue to give you little things like canapés; they are the subtleties you need to get full with

Every moment will be sweet as my charms, and every day I will unwittingly celebrate our amity

Because the joy inside of me feels like the way I cherish having a red cherry on my chocolate sundae.

Prima Donna, let me assail you with Hors d'oeuvre commingled with my pure gifts of humor and wits
Certain flowers when they bloom, they hold transcendences for charm and connection
Just as am assured that when I drink this vervain herb it will bring me good luck, virility and protection.
My Hors d'oeuvre is sprightly full of charms and ecstasies, a little here to make you fain; and small bits
Of it will macerate your unwitting heart to trust me the more. And now that you have this reflection
It gives me the courage to desire something this ethereal, and this endearing feeling is so
Satisfying like the taste of a Vacherin Mont d'Or.

My Hors d'oeuvre takes me to a higher plain; it's like watching the stars far above my reach in the sky
Even at my best, I still ponder if my Hors d'oeuvre can be as effervescent as your sensuality
It makes your smile to assail me the more to see your uniqueness and beauty,
I have such a big faith in my Hors d'oeuvre right now to do the impossible because this task
Making you mine will never stop, and it's an endless pursuit of happiness.

Grunge Style

This hind is bestowed with heavenly poise that stays strong forever.
She is enamored on each side of her hips by angels that protect her coyness from every hand
that tries to move forward to touch, and from every hand that reaches to caress it, however,
her beauty is hidden in her grunge style -clothing, her baggy clothes make her look rough and command
You to respect her hidden sensuality, but you just need to sally and open her up like a rough oyster shell.
Inside of her, she holds a special cream that serves as rich liquor for some men, and others
just see her loveliness as an assortment of Charcuterie inviting to the eyes and soul
Others might just feel a bit timorous as they unconsciously mention your name into the wind
They also believe they can surmount your derriere; I just watch them and laugh.

My beloved, am ready at anytime to show you my avowal and how much I respect your grunge style
I'm by the ceiba tree to get inspiration on how to propel your clam to receive me whole.
Anytime I dream of eating Cendol, I get all the subtleties of your affection in my mouth and then smile,
After a while, you can begin to see how my waist will be genuinely moving out of control,
it comes so natural anytime we come close without any space in between us
This round of rendezvous keeps happening anytime I dream of eating Cendol.
I know you are saying even in my grunge clothes I still slay and turn heads around,
even with my mélange appearance I still rock.
My beauty is hidden in grunge clothes, it hides my sensuality, and all a devoted man needs to do
is to sally me and open me up like a beluga fish, inside of me is the taste of Almas caviar
As long as there is no distance between us, I will always moan to your touch even in my grunge
It means then that I should move much closer to you and satisfy your undying desire.

Golden Lion Tamarin

Now that you are with me, I can hardly resist the fine color of your hair
I'm sure the smell of it is like the savor of emmental cheese
I adore the color of your hair and how it makes you look so divine and fair;
My darling, the color of your skin is fine like that of a Golden Lion Tamarin at ease.
I cherish our relationship and the quest to have you close to me is never going to stop.
I'll be peripatetic about it, and follow you from place to place to find solace in your breast
I will go to the highest mountain and steppes of the world to declare my love for you

As long as sunbirds can still break into the spathe of flowers and draw out their juices
I will conquer all that stands in my way to make you my lover and queen
Everything about you ignites passion deep inside of me, that's why my mind refuses
To calm itself and my verve about you is readily and easily seen.
I will forever enjoy touching your spotless skin so fine as that of a Golden Lion Tamarin.
These will be some of my ardent reasons why I want you here with me always
I need an insight into what makes your skin so rich and seductive.

Bel Air '57

Make me an unalloyed promise that will be smooth looking as my Bel Air '57
This kind of committal is what could easily make our hearts to suddenly connect
Because it's quintessential of all promises, I want you to take this committal seriously
I will also bring you something of substance that will equate with your unalloyed promise to me
That way, I will relinquish my selfless love to you and it cannot be measured.

Make me an unalloyed promise that is elegant as my Bel Air '57
Because am still having these mesmerizing thoughts of you dancing with me
I will let you French kiss me; a harbinger of sweetness it will be and it will surely refresh your soul.
You are still a dream to me; when you hold me in your tight hugs I just succumb to your warmth
This will make any man jealous when they see me poised to kiss you in a redolent way
I am all yours, and am willing to surrender to your nightly pleasures tonight.

Make me an unalloyed promise close to perfection as my Bel Air '57
Nothing is more fetching than this moment we are sharing
The thought of consummating our love with you in satin sheets is a promise that resonates in my head
I look at the Bel Air '57; I know you compare my physical attributes to its big tail side,
My Bel Air '57 looks like my big backside and it's swaying to the rhythm of my swell songs to you.
And since you have your fine silk shirt on with its brilliance turquoise color like that of my Bel Air 57
I will be the paramour you just keep being my lothario lover.

Nature Boy

Have you seen the rays of sunshine coming through the branches of dry autumn trees?

It feels like the unsung glory of an unpolished emerald, but when it's cleaned,

It holds picturesque dreams and looks divinely presentable.

Have you felt the pleasure of seeing the courtship dance of pheasants?

It enthralls the soul and conveys unalloyed feelings to my loins.

I've tried to reach you and bring some of the withal of Yosemite to captivate you with

I know it gave you great desires for me.

Once in my command, I'll be able to tell you to do something unsuided to me.

Seemingly, I want to dance like the pheasant and show you my polished emerald,

I believe these quaint subtleties will conquer you and move me closer to your heart.

Naturally, I want to breach out to you and kiss you like a dolphin coming out of the ocean smiling.

Nature Boy, your presence is more welcome than the burst of spring rain to calm my spirit

I promise you, I will give you my love because I trust you, and my name on your lips will be more

Fetching than seeing mountain goats gaily dressed in winter coats.

You are always in my mind that's why I try to traverse up as a snow leopard on a mountain

Yet I couldn't, but now am going beyond penchant levels chasing you wherever you run to,

even up the steepest rocks, across gorges so high above, and the look is leaving me breathless.

But, I will not stop because I want you by all means to be mine.

I want to try another offering and sing to you all of life's rhapsodies if I can show you some of my gifts -

If I can open up my hands like a magician and let monarch butterflies come out of them and swirl around

You, I know you will get moved to my attraction and pray to heaven to make you my Nature Boy.

Narwhal of the Pulpit

People called you the Narwhal of the pulpit, forbid me to say, why not?
The messages you convey and your presence always shone like the tusk of a narwhal.
And when you break out in songs, you danced like David danced when you're preaching;
Because you know in your heart that is the only way you can be seen breaching.

People called you the Narwhal of the pulpit many in disbelief try to compare others to you,
We laugh in jest because we all know you were the best!
The praises and songs you sang daily in the sanctuary made you always happy
Everyone came to sought you out for your wise counsel, you were indeed full of zest
For the work of God which made humanity value you as the Cullinan diamond.

People called you the Narwhal of the pulpit, in continuous admiration you taught us to be peaceful.
And most importantly, you never forgot to bring your family, kindred and neighbors to God.
Your preaching conveys faith, joy, hope, love, and peace, it resonates the salvation of Christ
That you carry deep within, and the smoothness of your voice is like a french breche de benou marble.
But you fought not to give us your belief but of salvation and love for one another,
Your fight was always on how to be saved in righteousness.

People called you the Narwhal of the pulpit because your true life stories were always relished,
You were deeply loved and everyone laughed at your tales, but why so soon O Man of God?
We know every man must take this voyage; we are in disbelief that you left us now
But we are grateful that your tusk was removed by God who has made us cherish you the more
Everyday your songs and tusk still communicate to us in tandem, and we see it and rejoice.
Narwhal of the pulpit you are enmeshed with the stars.

On My Own

If I can command one thing to disappear it will be the thoughts of us vacationing in Budapest

If only I can erase this grief that weighs me down now I will praise God's name

I want to remove the echoes of throes and the throbbing pain your love has caused me

You have left me with despair, and my heart is completely twain from so much pain

I'm all on my own, I'm scared of the nights, and I'm lonely and still hungering for your touch

Just seeing you brilliantly looking like a monarch butterfly moving freely away from our home

To chase worldly subtleties and enchanting waterfalls that don't hold substance gets me angry

How lucky you are, and how you can just forget our memories and promises.

But I can't do as well, I felt crushed by the penchant of your voice, it always sways my thoughts

To accept you into my soul, mind and heart at will.

Even though I hope for my heart to suddenly heal from how badly abraded you left it

You are leaving me to be on my own, I will not fight the temptation of seeing us together again

Even in my dreams and lonely hours, I still long for you and your affection

I will fight the temptation of indulging myself in the Eszterhazy Torta we both love to eat

Because that will only add to my instant happiness but it won't bring back your presence in my life.

Black Pearl of the Caspian Sea

Listen to every word that I say, I promise to conquer you with life's splendor

I have an insatiable appetite for you; it's just like having beluga sturgeon caviar everyday

You are so heavily endowed with life - endearing pleasures, which make my heart surrender

I look at your derriere as the Cullinan diamond rounded up nicely in everyway

You are my vision; you are the gift that I have received from the goddess Amphitrite

My only believe is that having you here with me is like an afterlife in the Elysian Fields.

I know seeing you daily was prurient enough for me and it has altogether vanquished me,

But the worst of it that always conquers me is the taste of your body, it's like Almas caviar!

That's why I treasure you; those are the reasons why I call you the Black Pearl of the Caspian Sea.

Resplendent Quetzal

Some guys may try to whistle subtleties to you like a narwhal to get your attention
I didn't need all that; I saw your fascinator at the wedding and became instantly enamored,
It regales you as a bird of paradise flower; it completely gave me a new dimension.
My intent is pure, which also help built up my confidence, and instantly my mind clamored.
This situation may look crazy to you, but I swear I will use it to my advantage.
There may be many who want to lek with me, but what do you desire?
Forget all those who have tried to show you charms and chivalry, and even offered you Gruyère cheese

I will take my devotion high because your beauty took my whims away to another level,
I am the debonair gentleman with valor; I am the one with the fedora hat on loving you from a distance,
You can call me your Resplendent Quetzal because I have everything that has transcended me
Forget all those who have tried to show you charms and chivalry, and even offered you Gruyère cheese
I don't like their attributes and all that they have gathered for the soi·rée just to contend with me.
Let me offer you a boudoir session after this event, only for this sole reason you will be acquainted
With all that is in my heart and what has transcended me into a Resplendent Quetzal.

Eureka - I am Yours and You are Mine

I saw you in a thousand dreams and even took you to the theatre
To listen to a symphony of violinists playing Eine Kleine Nachtmusik
Now that we are here, seeing the stars in your abalone eyes makes me shudder
am vanquished by the lights coming out of your shimmering eyes and the renaissance music.
I've dreamt of many ethereal things, and felt some sensations in my stomach
I've stayed in fate, relinquished my hope, forebode the desire of ever having happiness
But when I saw swans in the River Thames courting in evocative ways, it reinvigorated me
It compelled me to accept my fate, to hold on and keep on trying to make you mine.

I've always believed that seeing the stars in your eyes will be enough to make me shudder
I longed just for a day like these when I can be seen walking by your side with gaits
At the end of it all, I've trusted God for this blessing because you are my bread and butter.
I will remain prayerful, I will continue to pursue you, and I will never give up on this chase
Eureka, others that have come to lek with me daily will finally grow weary from despair,
And sooner or later their distorted faces will begin to look like they have rigor mortis
They treasure the thought of having your coyness, which I know they can never have because
they want an already built reservoir abundant to taste from.
It's still too drawn away and only a gentleman with pure intent will be the one you surrender to

Eureka, you are my perfect stream, one flowing with relish over the stones and leaves
It's like listening to a symphony of violinists playing Eine Kleine Nachtmusik
That's why I will patiently wait for you, as if slowly going through a fjord to enjoy all is beauty
As I enjoy this transcendence, I know you are about to bloom like the Queen of the Night
Nothing else will matter, it will just be the two of us enjoying life's precious moments
A bridge has been created in my mind and it's burning with desire, linking my heart to yours
As we listen to the symphony of violinists playing Eine Kleine Nachtmusik.

Goodbye Liverpool

To be honest, when faced with complex numbers I use to make jest of myself before, most especially when am solving mathematics but not anymore
My father has instilled into my core the solution of solving mathematics; thanks to him this has become my requital for all I've become today.
Those days I could hardly understand the steps and process he uses to arrive at answers
It's like trying to understand the love my father has for his beloved city, Liverpool

In solitariness, I've wondered what days like these will be when you are gone but not anymore
Because my childhood is now playing right in front of me since you've been gone, Daddy
I've playfully chased you around a thousand times in my dreams and will now have to laugh without you
I thank God I have all the ensemble of your characters, you have instilled all your virtues into us
And it assays the strength of your love for us all and the community you were part of

Daddy, you don't need to go around your favorite city Liverpool anymore in days and seasons
From up above, you have the means of seeing the unsullied imagery of the city you so much admire
And you can listen to the songs you love from the churches and be part of the celestials
That's why every one of us will continue to patiently follow your footsteps of selflessness and service
As if slowly going through a fjord to learn the vicissitudes of life's journey and the splendid settings of
Your beloved city Liverpool.
Goodbye Liverpool, my father's favorite city.

Kayan

Most notably, you can see the fine neck rings adorning my long neck
My fine appearances with you every now and then made everyone think we are good
But in reality, am carrying much deeper pains with my beautiful stretched neck
The mental, physical and emotional abuse I go through with you is endless
It has stifled my voice from crying out; I wish so badly to cry out for help
Since our avowal started, like a lark I was singing to the world the joy of our splendors and anecdotes
Maybe that is my shame today, every subtlety that you killed, every joy that I've ever known,
And all the enchantments of praises that made me bloom like the azaleas
During our courtship are now empty words full of bloviated tales.

I promised to give you every sweet part of me; it could have been like you having foie gras
And tasty macarons whenever you wanted me,
You would have enjoyed every substance of beauty enshrined inside of me because am full of wonders.
I dare you to take off my neck rings, and I will speak about the domestic violence I suffer in your hands
I know the world listened to my stories when I told them how incredible you made me feel
Likewise, I am ready today to tell the story of how you are a narcissist,
And all your redolent mannerism is just a smoke screen to your true character.

I've never seen such contrast of pain and pleasure; I know I still look beautiful with my brass coils
But it has stifled my voice long enough from crying and speaking out
I have everything that would have crowned you the king of my heart, just like I love to run my fingers
Through the afro hairstyle on your head, a crown you wear like a Napoleon wrasse
But instead you want to be a lothario; all you give to me are lies and the worst kind of abuse
if you think adding more coils to make my neck to make it elongated the more will make you reach
Higher heights of abuse, you are mistaken. I am just like a beautiful giraffe grasping leaves
From the tallest of trees and showing you my eyes are seeing new things happening in the world today.

Confusion

From the beginning of our relationship, I had the believe that I have a perspicacious mind
But loving you and waiting for an equal requital from you gets me very confused
Should I turn to my right or left, should I turn around and go backward, am I blind?
If I tarry here and wait for your move, I may end up getting bruised and misused
Should I titter here with you until heaven's light adjures your character to treat me right?
I cannot take all your deceits anymore, the weight of your unanswered response
Has pulled me down and left my addled brain muddled.
The effect of your incongruence brings me no delight.
I pray you make up your mind if you want to be with me or not.

Once again, I feel pushed out, and I looked through the windows of my house
To look for signs, to see if our stars are aligning, to fathom if I'll ever be your soul mate
To my surprise, a western meadowlark is on a tree, and I'm pulled to its songs to douse
My perspiring heart from burning over, I will never relinquish my hope of finding my ideal mate.
I am filled with your lies; it's as if I was gavaged by all your attributes and fairy tales you fed me with
I've found a resolution while driving through the high cliffs of Positano, the streets have an end after all
My clouds of despair are suddenly going away, and new insight is coming to me, no matter what
This confusion will pass, and I will finally have my defense to walk away from you.

Aurora

I will be on Amalfi Coast in the cool of the evening patiently waiting for you by the seaside

My ardor for pleas is already echoing around the cliffs and my voice is unmistakably confident

It has been shown to me that there will be a requital, that's why I can't wait for us to sit side by side

To say you are a heavenly beauty means I'm putting in an effort not to describe you as a monument.

When I saw you coming I recognize the color of love; I know you have on a pair of Manolo Blahnik heels

I've taken a fondness to the sprightly colors of summer you like to wear and the way you smell

I have looked into love's eyes and I've seen the treasures of its rhapsody and what it reveals

If you've ever wondered if a flower clock has its langor then we are in the same swell.

I've made songs about you that came to me in my dream; I have it all written down

I've seen the way your derriere moves like that of a halibut; this has held me in askance

Aurora, if passion is all that you desire, look towards me to give it to you tonight

Let's cherish the Tiramisu and all the other subtleties that have made you a wonder to me.

The Warrior (Osibisa)

Tonight, I will lek with your other suitor till we all run out of wits and disperse

I will return in the morning to defend my honor with all the rhapsodies and get you thrilled

While he scrambles for words to use, believe me, you will not be able to count my verses,

It will be strumming out of me because am an inveterate lover, I am highly skilled!

I am my strength; unlike him, that is laddish with his group of friends gathering at the Labadi beach.

All noise makers, are like sellers with no wares to sell at the Makola market

I can advise him to come with his support, whatever courage you have will be stolen from you tonight

When you see me coming, it will be like a conquistador.

We will fight from the rocks of Paga Nania to the Guelta d'Archei

I have the courage and a heart of a beast because fate has instilled inside of me courage

I will be victorious; that's why you will see me after this celebrating our amity all week long

I'm already having some local liqueur of Umqombothi with my lady and a dessert of Mandazi

Tomorrow we will be having Wasawasa and Kashata for dessert

And after that, we will be having fufu and soup and M'hanncha for dessert.

Do you honestly think that you have the withal like me to satisfy and conquer her?

You are already enamored by my personae, especially by my style and outfit that looks intriguing to you like the curved horns of a Markhor.

They will be like darts blinding your senses as I pull out my weapon.

Cruising (Smokey Robinson)

Think twice before you take this cruise with me to Marseille

Because the only sound you will be hearing will be the sweet sounds of the sea,

And the happy look on my face will be an endearment to you, it will make you weigh

Your decision if you are ready to take this cruise with me. But I already foresee

Us having a committal that will be unrivaled, my inkling tells me to go further and kiss you

I can go step by step to describe how enchanted the night has been to me,

This isn't perfidy; the night only holds what we both desire to do, and that is

To cruise and be free with each other, let us enjoy our romance.

I have unfettered lines to splurge you with along with some colorful Macarons

I can judge by the end of tonight, you will want another cruise with me

Breathe my love; open your eyes to see how I passionately stare at you when talking

I'm taking a stance with you, I am here to stay and enjoy life's splendor with you

Wherever you want to go, I'll be chivalrous and drive you to the best places in the world

To the Château de Versailles to get the feeling of how valiant men courted ladies

Whatever you want to dine with my love I will provide, I will make you the best meal

We can have dover sole meunière with some white Bordeaux wine tonight

I want this rhapsody to continue to echo in your mind and heart

I wish for your trellises to be wet with perspiration by the time we are back to our room

I desire for there to be an endless whisper that you are sliving and I've made you my Queen.

Saturn Return

I'm sliving, not because I asked for it, but because it's my Saturn return
My mannerism has changed to show my next stage in my growth and life
I am like a stimulating primrose showing the vicissitudes of life in turn
My thoughts have progressed to something heavenly without strife
I've set myself free from the chrysalis I was hiding into this new phase of life
I cannot say I'll be dutifully calm with my request to taste life's splendor
I'm ready for a lilt of sunshine to drive away this shadowy cast of forlornness
I'm ready to twirl about my evolvement, and am fain because I cherish it
I have a reassuring hope that I'm in a new haven and heavily blessed
Take me out of the unknown maze and bring me into this effervescent light
What I've needed all along was to be taken out of my pomace, it will change
The riveting state of my being to become alive and sensual, and that's why
am luxuriating with my Saturn return.

Set Me Free

Many times, I've brought forward my effects to you with my words and actions
Disdained by your lack of intimacy and respect for my being I've decided to move on
By the time I finish explaining my disavowal to you, you will understand my sudden reactions
Saddened by your lack of interest, passion and desire for my being I want to move on
This treacherous climb has left me running away from you like a mountain goat evading a predator
I want you to set me free instead of making me live my life the way you like to control it
I hope you set me free from your non -committal, misogynistic and egocentric behaviors
That way someone else will find me, and I could be remembered like the Winged Victory of Samothrace.

Sword of Damocles

I know certain things I've done to you will urge your heart to treat me with kindness
I gave you a tawny tennis bracelet to hold all my promises to you and to stop any mutterings
You are beautiful, and every day different suitors try to overturn me with their politeness,
Impressing upon your heart that they can give you finer things of life better than my offerings
By my reconnaissance, I now know that I have to be watchful, prayerful and hopeful!
And every day my words should not only hold true to you cause of all that I've promised to give to you
I desire for my words to be reassuringly refreshing as the sorbet you are relishing in your hand
Nothing distresses me more than seeing you walking alone on the promenade getting all this attention
So many characters, so much redolent eyes pleading with you to give them a chance
It's so bad that once your postings are on Instagram and Facebook, they are sliding into your DM
And leaving you comments on how they will always be there for you and love you the right way
They keep on showing you their nice sports cars with brilliant colors, and this annoys me
Even show you vacation trips, resorts, and spas they want to take you to
Promises of foods I've only dreamed about to dine you to, including Lobster thermidor and Canapé
With long essays of what they can assay you with, with diamonds and designer purses they can give you
In this new world, having a beautiful woman is like having the Sword of Damocles over your head.

Shiitake Mushrooms

I dreamt of a showdown of reverie with you that's why I came up with the ploy

of making you sautéed shiitake mushrooms with stir fries

I want to get you talking tonight; I'm starting you off with a Lillet Rosé aperitif to enjoy

It will melt your heart to have the desire for me, and then I will finally have my prize

I know that once you start tasting my shiitake mushrooms our rendezvous will begin

The décolletage dress you have on aptly tells me I won't find it easy taking my eyes off your chest

That's why I also made you my specialty salad with a nice Vinaigrette dressing to enliven your mind

I knew once you see and have a taste of it, our night will all be memorable

It's inescapable not to notice your brilliant smiles and affectionate ways toward me now

It just confirms everything I've long known that my shiitake mushrooms can let you undress for me.

Chants of Euphoria

In so many ways, I'll like to describe your affection for me as fleeting

I am in deep thoughts every day as if heavily enmeshed with the mizzles

That will soon transcend into summer rain while am planning for our meeting.

Sofia, I call you my muse as I stare into the candor of the night and see many men whistles,

Other great people partying on the deck of the cruise ship as we sail away to Florence,

It moves my soul to quickly unfold all my fondness to you as we are sharing kisses,

On the pool chairs, laughing, holding hands and sipping on our juice watching the night's performance.

Leonardo, every day with you is filled with splendor and magnificent mysteries
I am your muse, tell me how I delight your senses and how I've made you happy
If the opportunity this moment brings is anything to be joyous about, then serenade me!
I'm trying to en shield myself from getting disappointed by the degree of your burning words
I also have to transcend my swells to grow with you because that's where my destiny is.
But, since I am saving myself for the true gentleman that will sweep me off my feet
You have to keep on echoing your chants of euphoria to me to ignite my desire for you.

Sofia, thank you for making me unfold how madly I'm in love with you
I will sing of my fondness for you, I will chant my thoughts of rhapsody for you -

      I have lasting swirls inside of me that are bigger than the bevy of birds in the sky

      My feelings for you are more radiant than the shoal of thousands of fishes in the sea,

      And my emotion is running wild like the migration of wildlife in the Serengeti.

Since we are here, let me start by ascribing to you some of the many wonders I've seen in Roma
I've seen lasting art works in the Vatican museums, even the paintings of the creation –
These are ensembles that no one can ever doubt or judge their provenance
Some statues of the goddess Aphrodite are made of marble, others made with frescoes and rugs.
Sofia, if marbles are the lasting materials in this world to make perfect art work,
I will have them build me something to compliment your beauty, poise, and your grace
it will transcend my enduring love for you and be an everlasting monument that towers high
It's as if these swells and euphoria have been in me all my lifetime, waiting to come alive for you.

Leonardo -

You say that you have lasting swirls inside of you that are bigger than the bevy of birds in the sky
   That your feelings for me are more radiant than the shoal of thousands of fishes in the sea,
   Also, your emotion is running wild like the migration of wildlife in the Serengeti
Now that you've spoken such profound words to me, I want to be present in your life,
I want to speak such reassuring sweet words of hope and comfort to you.
Transcended by my joyous swells, I can no longer hide how crazy am in love with you too.
When we were at Ponte di Rialto, and walking on the street with the cobblestones, Allora
I got mystified by the sounds and vision surrounding me,
I could hear the chants/greetings from everyone who thought of us as lovers saying hello Signora!
Leonardo, the sweet echoes of people walking around at the San Lorenzo market has conveyed
Insatiable thoughts of you in my mind, and its driving me crazy!

Sofia, I must confess, you are the transcendent swells I saw in Florence and all of Roma,
Walking by your side, I see your svelte body as a curved cannoli, its breathtaking how your figure
is well accentuated nicely like the rusticated stones at the Medici Riccardi Palace, Allora
I believe when we get to the open colonnaded court in the Medici Riccardi Palace
I will continue singing my sweet songs to you, and I hope that it will make our hearts beat as one
I will stay with you forever because my euphoria ambles with yours, it only means splendor for us
Sofia, your dress and hair accoutrement is enchanting like the gallery at the Palazzo Vecchio,
Your posture is like the swells at the Piazza del Signoria, that's why every hand wants to touch you
Sofia, at the Piazza del Duomo, believe me, I saw the semblance of seeing heaven on your face
When you were looking up and staring at the cathedral, I swear, I almost saw you as ecclesiastical,
And all that lasting ensembles that you carry glisten from you and it holds me spellbound
It has given me a new meaning, in my eyes and in my heart
You are my Transcendent Swells and I'll forever chant euphoric songs to you.

Beauty is Only Skin Deep
(The Temptations)

Since am in Marseille, I can let go of my frigidness and fall in love with my French lady

What enamored me about you, is your sweetness; it's rich as a Chocolate Mousse,

I will settle for how you look now because I know inside of you lay unseen treasures to sway me

I want to build on the reverie and compassion you showed me the very first time we got introduced

If I take this quest seriously, I will one day be the beau to her deserving heart

Other men may want it differently than me and go for the slim ladies with thigh gaps

But don't forget, these are unseen gold diggers traversing the California Rodeo walk, and many

Are in a ménage à trois relationships seeking only riches and pleasures

Because you see her in the best of designer labels and bikinis it doesn't mean she is good

I tell you, unseen gold diggers keep selling you debauchery that feels like soul food

Even if she twirls and makes your mind go crazy like the taste of a Fleur burger,

Stay strong brother, and don't be moved by all the showy thongs her big arse can't hold in

Please don't lose your senses over Hermes and Birkin bags, also her smooth legs without cellulite,
Especially the ones with the flat bellies and string monokinis, I know they are very enchanting
Try reaching out for something more divine and true, something that truly holds its value
Because beauty is only skin deep and the desire to have a beautiful woman never ends.
I want something deeper than a woman's beauty; a lady that will stand by me and support me
I need something more flavorful in her character and understanding.
I hope to find a woman that stays pure through the season, and believes in me
I saw one at the Marinha beach and her behavior and persona say it all
She had her hair coiffed; she held my breath that I almost collapsed
Beauty is only skin deep, you have to get it right so that you can enjoy the essence of it all.

Livin' la Vida Loca

Last night, I got a ting from your glamorous lifestyle at the Serendipity,
It makes me wonder if my withal is strong enough for me to exult about my admiration
and affection for you. Let me calm my verve because I see you are looking at my sensitivity.
Your steps on the dance floor are soughing a sensation for me to sprightly start up a conversation
you are my heartthrob tonight, you are the queen of my heart - bésame
I can breathe your candor and relish the thought of buying you a blue haven
Everything about your taste and style looks expensive like Frrrozen Haute Chocolate ice cream sundae
And right now, it's been splayed on my mind to endlessly pursue you

Your wild lifestyle has stirred me in no easy manner it assays me to observe and speak the truth
of your wildness as the living d'origine controlee, even your burning blue eyes just make me marvel!
The swishing sounds you made with your risqué entrance only made me smile at your grandeur
Mi amor, something about you just resonates with those wild dreams I used to have of
partying with a coquette lady like you.
Something in me hope that you can be gravid and something in me also hope that
we can find something to expiate this attitude from you, that way you will slow down
But, I know you like the joie de vivre of life too much for you to slow down.

Who Do You Love – Bernard Wright

I am not blindsided, and I definitely cannot call or accept this ménage à trois

All along I planted subtleties that could easily conquer any wench

I may be impecunious to your standard, but I've got so many virtues that make me

To be a worthy lover and a potential husband for you

All this time I've been with you, you are still undecided on who to love,

Who do you love? It's like me asking you which dessert you prefer the most

    Is it the Cornes de Gazelle or the Baklava,

    Is it the Crème Brûlée or the Gâteau Fondant au Chocolat,

    Baby, as long as your bodycon dress is enduringly showing all your curves

    I'll be dying to share every moment of my life with you.

You can't even imagine the magnitude of my avowal toward you in my Calabasas home

In my mind, loving you is like a dive into the Rio Celeste or having a taste of Tequila Komos

It's sensual; it changes and takes the depth of my thoughts to a higher heaven

Who do you love? Just like tasting your favorite food and having it at all times

I want to know which dessert you prefer the most after your meal

    Is it the Cornes de Gazelle or the Baklava,

    Is it the Crème Brûlée or the Gâteau Fondant au Chocolat,

    Baby, as long as your bodycon dress is enduringly saying to me baby come to me

    I will follow the fullness of the moon to the Rio Celeste there we can be au naturel.

Turquoise

Why does the color turquoise make you bloviate?

I know you like everything you have on to amble with your turquoise dress

The magic and the mood created by it have everyone enamored, and yes, it's very appropriate!

You call it a sensational color; I see everyone's feeling is affected by your carriage and finesse

It's unbelievable how the color of the water ambles swiftly with your turquoise dress

We are in Sanctuary Cap Cana; I can taste the brilliance of the sun on the water

And, surprisingly, you alone have that color on, it's like le Privilège du blanc

Given to you alone, you have this freedom to slay every onlooker.

I feel like nothing is more special or beats the ensembles of your turquoise dress

It evokes such delightful pleasure just like visiting the Rio Celeste River

It's an unexplainable thrill to see you outdoors showing everything you possess

I can imagine having a semblance of you as a pet to stay indoors with me to make me quiver

I will have you as my pet, like an Arowana in an aquarium cause of your noblesse

I can't wait to see you jump into the sprawling pool, that way every splashing move you make

And the evocation of your trellises resting nicely on your head will be too much for me

to carry within and this will send an unseen jolt to my sensibilities.

Trevi Fountain

It was an amicable agreement for us to visit the Trevi Fountain for its astounding view
I so sought at that moment to throw some of the coins I had with me and made a wish
And magically, I was rewarded with some naked man orchid in my hands to give to you
This will amble with the au naturel statures at the Trevi fountain as they will make us flourish
Nothing in me wants to hold back, everything inside of me wants this to be true.
It can be a conjugal belief if you just look into my eyes and rehash our love
This was what we said last night that we hope for our love to be everlasting.

I am yet to return all the wits bestowed unto me about your eternal beauty.
There are things meant to be said under the Azure sky, ordinary things about our love
Have made us to be a power couple and we are here to rehash our commitment at the Trevi fountain
Where several lovers, bards, visitors, and the community can echo our prayers.
Swishing water sounds at the fountain are more enduring than the mellifluous songs of a Goldfinch
The epiphany I get seeing the fountain water flow keeps me subdued, am humbled by the belief
Millions of people have over its sacredness and the penchants for making wishes come true

Right now, just being close to you is sweeter than the sweet smell of muskoxen, and your eyes
are more radiant than the Illumination of the Cullinan Diamond.
Trevi Fountain is the raddest place to unfold our desire, and I will make my everlasting promise now
I wish for you to be transformed from just being glamorous to something ethereal like the Trevi fountain
I hope the ordinary things I brought to the fountain are enough to make you echo my cultivation
I pray nothing destroys our peace and everything in life makes us connected forever.
I cherish every moment with you and I know the heights of our affection are reaching for the stars.

Red Glasses

I wonder why am shivering and why I've got goose pimples all over my hands
I think it's because am staring at your loveliness on the deck and the way it makes me swoon
If I say am fain, it's because you have your red glasses on again and it ambles with my plans
Showing you off in your lacey slit Vera Wang gown, this will shut everyone up, even a typhoon.
The slit of your dress is so pretty high up that I can see your lovely legs and curvaceous body
If we remain on this cruise, other maenads may try to win my interest in their two -piece ensemble
But I have already made many acquaintances here that will defend your honor
I have friends that will echo your subtleties to remind me of my promise to love you endlessly.

Darling, I like your red glasses, since I call them my rhapsody on this delightful cruise
I will kiss you on your neck and cheeks because you are my queen, also I like the color of your rogue.
I hope am the most interesting person you can get attached to; I'll be the dos Equis for your night muse
I have nothing else to compare your red glasses with, other than the cabaret of the Moulin Rouge
You know how to conquer me with your alluring ways and stunning red glasses
I reckon you can give me a private show on the cabaret of the ship and show me some passion
I'm sipping my glass of vesper martini and waiting to enjoy my lobster thermidor dinner with you
I see this as a provocation and it will quickly help to arouse my mood for all the conquest tonight.

Lady Yas

Nothing is more charming than our endeavor to see the world together
Seemingly, I have promised to get you a Cane corso to protect you when you go outside
You will certainly win hearts when walking down the street in good or bad weather
Other admirers like to turn around and look at your svelte body on the roadside.
It's good to know they will be forever afraid to tell you their sordid tales and the fantasies they arbor.

Lady Yas, I know we will continue to move from one wonder to another like butterflies moving
Freely with so much allure, enjoying life splendors together
Although you've already judged me right, I'm your ariten ready to take you grooving
To all events, travels and parties from morning till evening in all weather
Because I cherish every moment being with you. I truly love you.
I wish I can learn the strumming sounds of the Swainson thrush and take all its songs
and sing them to you over and over again.

My Lover, to seethe my thoughts right, I have such desire to make you my soul mate
You will be eternally etched into my soul because am madly in love with you too
I am more determined to make you my life partner and husband; you are my fortune and best friend
The zest I have to see us succeed is stronger than the will of long-tailed ducks swimming to the highest
depths of the ocean bed to get mollusks.
In my mind, am ready to follow the sillage of your Baccarat rouge to climb the highest mountain top
To get the smell of you, your enduring words are tempting enough for me to think of you as my Elysian.

I believe every step of ours will be more regal than the colors of the Vatican Swiss guard's uniform
Lady Yas, honestly the vision I have for us is more enchanting than the Duin- en Bollenstreek
Believe me, our love will be eternal, it will be perfection, and it will amble with my dream of
Having a rendezvous with you, you can tell from the lilt I have up my spine like an art form.
The fervor of my affection for you is more exciting than shopping at the La Samaritaine,
and the thought of making memories with you lingers on longer than the taste of Chateau d'Yquem
Lady Yas, I love your svelte body and the way your curvaceous backside shakes,
Nothing can change my chargrin for you; even in the hottest Naica cave, I'll be there
In the ocean depths and in the coldest glaciers, I still want to be with you everywhere.
Call it all the trials of a romantic love interest for my temperate lady;
I always like to see you smile. I love you so much, in every way I adore you - besitos.

My lover, how pertly when I say this; I can affirm from my conviction that you are my best friend.
I know heaven heard me when I asked for help for the Alcázar of Segovia castle bridge to be closed
To keep other admirers out, I also prayed that side distracters be shut out, not to be able to attend
Any of my nuptials with you and walk in the park, nothing else will be showed
There is no way I'm missing out on anything out there because you are my fortune,
That is why am declaring it to the world, if life makes us swoon, we will do it together,
If I live long, I want it to be in your loving arms in any weather,
I'm in paradise with you. I love you so much too, in every way I adore you - besitos.

Madame du Barry

Everyone is welcome to celebrate this moment with me, nothing to worry about

my Dogue de Bordeaux are on standby to protect the court from truculent foes.

If they want to cast aspersion on your character, look away from them and have no doubt

I will be very chivalrous and gallant enough to set them right if they ever put their nose

In our business and talk about your background as being of lower class and loud,

Madame du Barry, I'm ready to show you off as my maîtresse-en-titre,

Among your greatest qualities you are considered an aficionada for the émigrés

Madame du Barry, let us walk our way into the garden and sit by the Apollo fountain

As I place my head close to your side fringe, the whole of Versailles will acknowledge our love.

From the moment we have been together, you have touched the soul of my being with your compassion

I will hold you up in high esteem, just like holding my arms to shore up the leaning tower of Pisa

Madame du Barry, I will take you to the court for the masquerade dance ball

Everything about us will be known when we take down our masks to show our faces.

At Last (Etta James)

At last, I finally have someone I can bring carnation flowers
I now understand how to unfold my admiration for you
And how to pleasure you into the midnight hours
At last, I have stopped my laddish ways; I only pursue what's true!
The innate core of my desire now is well -matured; it has given me such powers,
It has stopped me from chasing after endless dreams so that I don't follow through.
At last, I have someone I can share my desires with and talk to into the late hours
I am able to go shopping for my lady, and I got you a Pomsky to show you my love is true.

At last, I've replaced my emotions with inklings that show my sensibilities.
I am no longer looking for fine bodies and beautiful faces that are so untrue,
I am no longer prurient whenever I think of your svelte body and desirability
Though your attributes are to die for, I look deeper into my thoughts, I need to subdue
Anything that will make me not experience the true meaning of love and stability
At last, the storm inside of me is calm; I am no longer alone or lonely
Life has taken a significant new turn; I now have fairy tale stories of my own.

Sarah Baartman

In Marseille, by the Basilique Notre Dame de la Garde, something spurred
My senses see your loveliness and the reason why everyone talks about your derriere
Truth be told, I was enamored by the Madonna and child statue high up in the sky, I observed
Its magnificence and how enchanted the onlookers are just staring at it, I just stood still when there.
One thing that always leaves me breathless is the size and shape of your derriere
The curviness of your voluptuous backside takes the breath out of me, you can agree with my stare
I like your physical attribute, I can only describe how enamored I am, and it's like that of Sarah Baartman
Your words have found their way to the heart of my being, the sweetness of your love is enduring
Like the freshness of the breeze at the port and the lavender flowers adorning the city of Marseille.
Your chemise is piquant and your coiffed hair leaves me speechless like the taste of bouillabaisse
My memories of Marseille and fondness will always be your hips, and it's like that of Sarah Baartman
I tell myself beautiful lady, your curve is original. The best of the best, its je ne sais quoi.

Stomp

Since you were the one with the diamond chain and the see-through gown
I could only believe it was my chance tonight to cherish this very moment of chance meeting
While I can still believe the music will be swirling and make me declare what I've found
Nothing will stop me from going down on you and making you go on the ground kneeling
I love your lissome lips, svelte body, and your lovely shimmering eyes
When you see such an allure, you can steadily dance to the light her smile brings
This will be a rendezvous; I will not let you go before I see the world with you

I reckon we can continue to chill and relax; I will fly you to the reverie city of Las Vegas
We are in Las Vegas, neon lights everywhere; I feel your warmth as I sip on my glass of vesper martini
There will never be a dull moment, everything we do will make us laugh, and our dancing will be contagious
We can take turns to unfold our desires while cruising to the Cosmopolitan in my Huracán Lamborghini
People everywhere, the feeling on their faces is like the excitement at the white-pebble Lama Monachile
You and I won't be saying good night, I will be inviting you over to my place for a glass of vesper martini
Sweetheart, it will be morning before I let you go back home, I will be stomping with you all night long.

Hug

Let me hug you and make you feel the kind of love I have for Netherland
My ardent belief is that once I hold you close you will feel enamored by my embrace
Hurry up to me before the brilliance of the Tulips in the fields fades away into the night
Let me caress you and make you smell the musk oxen I have on, it assays
My burning desire for you, and I can't wait to kiss you on your lissome lips tonight
All I want to be remembered for is the infinite swells I gave to your heart for days

Open up the curtains, it's time for me to make my grand entrance
It's me, I can be aptly described as a chaste lady, and I've borne so much inkling
That has made me ready to live forever in your dreams, I urge you to follow my transcendence
I don't have to wonder anymore why you like twirling my Scarf a la creole in your hands singing
I like the candor of the evening, and seeing the bottle of D'usse Cognac XO in your hands is resplendent,
It only means one thing; I'll be in your hands enjoying the hugs you give to me.

Soul Man

He is always affluent when it comes to singing those soulful songs

His presence at an event could be more priced than the sweetest kobe beef

His ability to transform dull moments into reveries makes everyone drop their jaws

The tone of his voice is as smooth as a labradorite that sooths every grief

Have never seen such excitements like this whenever you come around, also the applause.

Some call you Junior; I call you Mr. Eddie for your ingenuity and many good qualities

The ladies always wait to feel the onslaught of sweet songs coming out from you and your

Nicely choreographed steps on the dance floor, cause it caresses their souls.

The guys are echoing your tones and equally behaving silly, the feeling it creates is joyous

It's like the effect of touching the right breast of Juliet in Casa di Giulietta.

After seeing this gossamer of wires around you, your opened eyes and non-responsive mouth

Nobody knows if you are going to stay with us or move on to the afterlife

Whatever the case maybe, the thoughts and loving memories of you will stay with us forever

It can never be erased; it is well preserved in our soul like storing seeds in the Svalbard global seed vault

Famine in Samaria
2 Kings 6:25-31 KJV

I thought once we are leaving the cold of the winter and about to enter summer

It will be eureka for everyone, everywhere will be full of life and the parks will be reopened again.

And instead of our children celebrating as if they are in Disney land, we are busy hiring drummers

For funerals, we are at the cemetery weekly, if not daily, burying one child after the other again.

Since your son and his gangs killed mine on the street, now my son's gang members and brothers

Will assert its own revenge and kill yours too, on the street or anywhere they find him

For sure they will find him when he is running away, hiding, in his car driving or with others.

This has already caused an estrangement, and the souls of our children are seriously damaged.

We have cried out on all the Media for it to convey our helplessness and grief to the world

So far, nothing seems to work because they are still very busy shooting one another,

The tears of parents, gun control measures, church preaching and all the other social programs created to stop this carnage has not worked.

I hope the heebie-jeebies am having about seeing our cities turn into ghost town stops

I pray our men find the fortitude to fight against hate and indiscriminate attacks on one another

Otherwise, they will end up killing everyone here, so that it becomes increasingly hard

To find anyone left in the city. Our situation is very dire, and soon it will be like the famine in Samaria where there was nothing else to kill and we will now have to agree on bringing our children out ourselves for them to be killed.

The roads are thirsty for blood; we will kill mine today and kill yours tomorrow.

Nightshift

I have good memories of your character and gentleness, and it's still as sharp as a Samurai sword
I still sit and wonder how you could go so soon when we already had so many plans
Your preaching at the pulpit is magnificent and it's something that will forever be explored
Your bible and the teaching manuscripts you left behind will be treasured by our hands
I hear your songs in my head all the time; your recitals are very quaint and will be in our record.
this generation adores you and the landmark things you put in place will be forever remembered

If anyone knew about cartomancy they would have done it then to avert this other grief
Nothing prepared our minds for Deacon Felix death, but in all we still give thanks to God
He was the local philanthropist known all over the country and in every church giving relief
To widows and children, he brought everyone into his house; this never seems to be an odd
Thing to do for anyone, he was a beloved character.
I know you are two beautiful endearing souls singing with the angels
I know you are both leading everyone to visit and converse with humans to save souls.

Barista

It's such a perspicacious belief that we know how to mix all the coffee
I like your trust in seeing me shake my cup and pour you out a deluge of combinations
Of treats, some sweet and some sour enough to inflame your senses and body
I may simply be your Barista, but I also like to meet people and make conversations
The favorite drink that I mix is the Caffe Latte with almond milk coffee
Everything is done according to your explanations and expectations.
I reckon I can be more than your Barista and friend; I will like to be your trophy.

The display of coffees is an accoutrement and my ability to mix it all together makes you rouse
With excitement when you see everything I put inside the cup swirling with perfection and love
My job is to make little pert conversations with you, make you smile and reminisce in my coffee house,
The coffee gives you the belief you have serendipity because of the way you take of your gloves
To feel the warmth of the cup, and after you take a sip there is this unseen lilt in your blouse
Everyone calls what I do showmanship, and how I make them feel inside a masterpiece.
I reckon I can be more than your Barista and friend; I will like to be your trophy.

Printed in the United States
by Baker & Taylor Publisher Services